DEVELOPER RELATIONS FOR BEGINNERS: WHAT TO KNOW AND HOW TO GET STARTED

Sarah Lean

Copyright © 2021 by Sarah Lean

All rights reserved. No part of this book may be used or reproduced in any manner without written permission from the publisher, except in the context of reviews.

All trademarks are the property of their respective companies.

Dedicated to the people who love me for who I am.

Welcome

Thank you so much for picking up a copy of **Developer Relations for Beginners: What to Know and How to Get Started.** I'm so glad you are here!

This book is my way of giving back to the IT community, of helping those that are interesting in getting into Developer Relations understand what it is about. Sharing experiences, I have had over the last few years working within that side of the IT industry.

Developer Relations is one of those terms you might have heard mention on social media or even a conference and it sounds sweet right, getting paid to learn, teach, create content and potential travel. But what does it actual entitle, what does it mean for your career and what will your daily and yearly challenges be?

This book explores what Developer Relations is and what real purpose it has for the IT community as well as an organisation.

It also tackles the question about whether it's only for Developers!

And last but not least it tackles some practice advice on how to get started as an Advocate and things to consider if you are looking to pursue it as a career path.

I hope you enjoy this book; it has been a wonderful experience trying to put my thoughts and experiences down on "paper". I created this book to help so I would love to hear your thoughts and feedback. Please do reach out.

Cheers!
-Sarah Lean

https://www.techielass.com
https://www.x.com/techielass
https://www.instagram.com/_techielass

Table of Contents

Chapter 1: What is Developer Relations? 10

Chapter 2. Purpose 15

Chapter 3. Do you have to be a developer to work in Developer Relations? 20

Chapter 4. What makes up the Developer Relations department? 22

Chapter 5. Advocacy Job Titles. 27

Chapter 6. Metrics 29

Chapter 7. So, you want to be an advocate? 31

About The Author 36

Chapter 1: What is Developer Relations?

I have been in the Advocacy arm of Developer Relations (DevRel) for more than two years. Through my own experience and research within the IT community and DevRel community I have produced my definition of what it is.

Developer Relations or DevRel as you will sometimes hear it referred to. Is the department within a company that handles building or helping the community of users that have adopted your product or tool.

Every company will have their own goals or definition for Developer Relations. But broadly it should be about representing the external community. Helping to understand the mood of that community. Helping with product education or awareness.

It should be a two-way conversation though. Connecting the dots between the users of your product and tool and your company.

Under Developer Relations you will find Advocacy, Events, Community Management, Content, Documentation, and a lot more...

Every company will define their Developer Relations department differently. You may see variations on the above.

Developer Relations is a new term, but when we think of technical community engagement it has been around since the 50s or 60s.

As the IT industry has evolved, so has the terminology. So today technical community engagement is called Developer Relations.

For me there are four key principles that Developer Relations should revolve around, and this is what drives me.

Community - being involved, helping organise conferences or volunteering at user groups.

Awareness - helping to highlight your company's product or tool.

Feedback - taking feedback from the audience back to the engineering team and vice versa.

Education - helping audiences understand your product or tool. Answering questions and being one of the users contact points.

ONLY FOR DEVELOPERS?

One misconception I have seen is that Developer Relations is only for developers and that is not the case. Developer Relations is the industry term, but it does not mean it is only about talking to developers. It is about talking to the community, the audience, who use your product or tool.

For other organisations the audience will be quite extensive, covering developers, IT Pros, business decision makers, database administrators. And well, everyone else within the IT department.

It is about helping those that need help, regardless of their job title.

ADVOCACY

One arm of Developer Relations is Advocacy.

You will see those in Advocacy have job titles like, Cloud Advocate, Developer Advocate, Cloud Developer Advocate. We will dive more into job titles later in this book.

Those within the Advocacy role for their organisation will often be the most visible. They will be the people speaking at events, active on social media, the face of videos, etc.

TECHNICAL

Within the Developer Relations department to be successful I'm in the school of thought that there need to be a good range of people who have "been there and done it". And by that, I mean people who have worked in the IT industry and experience of working within IT departments. Seeing how it works outside of the technical documentation. People who have seen the dynamics of technology working when end users, budgets, time frames, etc are involved.

But increasingly I am seeing Advocates who are self-taught, who have worked hard to learn not a certain technology but have learnt how to be content creators in their bedroom.

Having a diverse group of people from different viewpoints, different learning paths, different journeys, adds value to your team.

There needs to be an element of your team who are technical, especially if your audience is technical. You don't just want people who are good at talking in front of an audience or are good copy writers in your team.

You want people who have the skills, experience, and passion to be out on that stage to help get your audience passionate about your technology or product.

But they also must have the "soft skills" in their toolset as well. Being able to relate to people, talk to them and understand how to communicate the knowledge across.

There's often a lot of talk about introverts and extroverts within the IT industry. Some of the best public speakers and people within Developer Relations I know are introverts. As I said if they have the skills, experience, passionate and "soft skills" to engage with the audience it doesn't matter if they are an introvert or extrovert.

WHAT IT ISN'T

Now that we have established what Developer Relations is, let us look at what it is not or what it should not be for an organisation.

It should not be about selling. It is about helping people to solve their problems or understand the use cases of a product or technology.

Depending on the company you either find the Developer Relations department sitting within the Marketing team or Engineering team.

Chapter 2. Purpose

As I mentioned in Chapter 1 for me Developer Relations focuses on four key areas community, awareness, feedback, and education. Let us take each of those and dive into them in more depth.

Community

"A community is a social group whose members have something in common, such as a shared government, geographic location, culture, or heritage."
- Definition from dictionary.com

That's the official dictionary definition of community. And I think it's pretty spot on in a general sense. I've found within the IT industry there is a great community spirit, there are always a few bad apples in the pile, but overall, everyone is nice.

I've also found that within that big IT community there are smaller communities. Communities that focus on a niche. That niche can be due to geolocation reasons. Or it could be because of product loyalty.

These communities either from other large communities or they grow organically.

The role of the Developer Relations department is to help those communities that are relevant to your company or product.

Helping can come in many forms. You could volunteer your time to help run the communities' meetups or events. You could provide sponsorship for them to cover food and drink at their events. You could help spread the word about the community through your social media networks. And endless more possibilities.

Your goal of helping the communities should be about fostering a good vibe. It shouldn't be about how many sales you can make or revenue you can generate from that community.

Fostering that good will and good vibe within the communities should lead to sales and revenue for your company. But the reason you help the community shouldn't be to get sales. The community will spot that, and you'll find that tactic will do more reputational damage than good.

Awareness

You might see awareness and think Marketing. And to be honest there is an element of that within awareness. But it is not your traditional marketing. Where someone in a Marketing Agency writes some copy, makes a graphic and that is turned into a billboard or a Tweet.

Raising awareness within Developer Relations is doing it in a much more natural, sympathetic, organic way.

A couple examples of that could be spending time on social media and forums answering questions from the community. Or celebrating the fact that community members are writing blog posts, sharing knowledge with others.

You do not always have to be the one creating the instructional video or blog post. If someone in the community has created a great bit of content, highlighting that, and sharing it can help to raise awareness. And build relationships.

FEEDBACK

Feedback works both ways. You want feedback on your product or tool from your customers. And you want feedback to go back from your company to your customers.

Feedback should be a conversation. Explaining your choices and understanding your customers or community's needs.

The Developer Relations department should be a conduit help that route that feedback. It should be more than just a messenger role though.

The Advocates for example should be close to your product or tool. They will have identified good and bad points about your product or tool. They can help to provide both empathy to the audience and provide a workaround. Or context on when the issue will be resolved, without breaking any Non-Disclosure Agreements (NDA).

If a pain point has been identified by the community but the engineering team are not convinced it should be a priority in their development cycle.

The Developer Relations department can help to gather feedback and arguments as to why it's such a major pain point for customers. And show why it should be considered a priority.

This work helps to not only build your own relationship with other teams inside your organisation, but it helps build up the trust of the community.

EDUCATION

Developer Relations teams should be focusing on educating their end users or potential end users.

Education can take many forms:

- Creating documentation or usage guides

- Speaking at events

- Being active on forums

- Delivering workshops

- Collaborating with community members

Your community will vary in how they want to learn about your product or tool, so you need to be prepared to go where your community is.

Experiment with social media platforms, with documentation, with video content. Try all methods available to you and see what receives engagement.

Remember though, education is not selling. It is about helping your community understand the product or tool and its usages. Solving their problems.

It might sound like awareness and education are the same thing. They are not.

Education is about teaching. Solving Problems. Helping.

Awareness is about brand recognition.

Chapter 3. Do you have to be a developer to work in Developer Relations?

The term Developer Relations or DevRel can be an alien one to anyone that is not a Developer. It can seem very exclusive.

For me, someone who has never considered themselves a developer. It has been hard working within a department, or industry that classes themselves as Developer Relations.

But it is getting better. People are starting to realise that even if Developer Relations was started to focus on the Developer Audience. There is so much more of an audience out there that needs love and attention.

Within an IT department, you will find a variety of job roles, Managers, Network Specialists, Infrastructure Specialists, Desktop Specialists, Security Specialists, Developers, Projects Managers and much more.

If your company is trying to convince IT departments to buy your product or tool, you need to think about the full conversation.

What questions or conversations should you be having with the Decisions Makers?

What does the conversation look like if you are talking to the Security Specialist?

You need to be ready and aware of the full conversation that will be occupying your customer when considering your product or tool. And be able to be a part of that.

Your Developer Relations department should have a diverse range of people. And by diverse, I mean people who have different skillsets.

Someone who is enthusiastic about security and knows that community and how to interact with them.

Someone who has infrastructure experience, knows the questions, and concerns other infrastructure specialists will have when they see your product or tool.

Having people who represent and are of a similar makeup to your customer will help you and your business. Conversations you have with your customers will be complete. You will not be missing a vital part of the conversation with your customer which could cost your business a sale.

Chapter 4. What makes up the Developer Relations department?

Every organisation will have a slightly different makeup to their department; however, I want to explore some of the core roles and responsibilities that often fall under the Developer Relations Department umbrella.

Advocacy

This is the part of Developer Relations you will most likely be most familiar with. As I said earlier the Advocates in your team will be the people speaking at events, active on social media, the face of videos, etc.

Your Advocates should be focussed on helping the end users, current and future ones. Helping to answer those questions the community has.

Your Advocates shouldn't just be content creating machines. They should be creating content that helps the audience, that answers questions.

Advocates can work with all different arms of the organisations, sales, documentation, customer success, marketing, finance…. They'll be collaborative and try and try to bring together different departments to make the most impact to the audience.

Advocates should be aiming to finding gaps and filling those gaps. Find the gap in your products. Find the gap between what your audience needs and what you do. Spend your time in the gap.

All too often Developer Relations departments confuse quantity over value. Over impact. What impact will this effort or project have?

We'll talk more about this in the Metrics section.

DOCUMENTATION

Not every organisation will have a full department or team dedicated to writing the documentation for their product or products.

Documentation is an important part to customers adopting your product. Without it they may struggle to implement it and make the best use of their investment.

The documentation part sits well within the Developer Relations umbrella for several reasons.

Technical documentation writing is about being able to convey messages and meanings across clearly and concisely to your audience. Developer Relations is also about getting that information across.

Also, one of Developer Relations missions is to seek feedback and hopefully action it. If your Advocacy team is collecting feedback about documentation being missing or not being comprehensive enough. It should be simpler for action to be taken if the Advocacy team and documentation team are within the same part of the organisation. Their missions and objectives are aligned, making it easier to collaborate. Or at least that is the hope.

EVENTS

This part of the department will look after organising first party events and look after aspects needed when attending third party events.

Organising a first party event can be a daunting process, there is lots of factor in, such as:

- Ticketing
- Advertising
- Speakers
- Catering
- Venue/Streaming platforms
- Timings
- And much more!

It can take an army to get an event off the ground and it can take months to plan. Having a dedicated team to run that is important.

Supporting a third-party event as a sponsor also can take lot of organising and logistics.

- Booth design
- Booth logistics
- Booth speakers
- Booth swag
- And much more!

Having people who understand the event space and how to run successful ones, either first party or third party can be crucial to achieving your organisational goals.

PROGRAM MANAGEMENT

This might come under a lot of different names, essentially it is the part of Developer Relations that helps to manage parts of the department.

You'll often seen regional program managers who are help support a specific geographical area. They'll help to coordinate and execute online and offline activities within the region. That could be helping with local content, regional blogs, and networking with local communities. They'll have a great understanding of the local region's needs and ecosystem.

Sometimes you'll find this is a technical role other times you'll find this to be a non-technical role. It can depend on the organisation. This could be a potential entry area for people looking to become Advocates.

Other responsibilities within the program management space could be:

- Creating processes around speaking at, attending, sponsoring events
- Creating onboarding documentation and processes for the Developer Relations team
- Helping to track and maintain metrics on the community
- Identifying risks and helping to remove any blockers
- Helping to use data to advise on decision-making

Your Advocates will be visible to your community but so will your Program Management team. They'll be the ones in contact with local user groups or conference organisers and will be that go to point of contact.

Chapter 5. Advocacy Job Titles

Job titles are one of those things that everyone says do not matter, but let's face it they do. They identify us to our colleagues and to our family. People can pre-judge you over a job title.

A recent search on LinkedIn found 91,000 people using the Developer Advocate job title. 112,000 people using the Cloud Advocate job title. The Cloud Developer Advocate job title threw back 29,000 people.

These are the most common job titles you will find being used by Advocates.

I've also seen titles like:

- Developer Educator
- Developer Relations Engineer
- Developer Experience Engineer

But there is a trend now of people using other job titles. Some departments are starting to use more traditional job titles to identify their Advocates.

And this stems unfortunately from bias towards the Advocacy job title or initiatives. There can be a lot of negativity around the Advocacy role and department as some people associate it solely with marketing and trying to sell you a product.

This is something to consider and make sure you are clear to define both internally and externally if you are setting up Advocacy within your organisation. Try and head off any pre-conceived notion that your team are a sales or marketing team. Ensure that they are identified as technical experts that can help the community.

Chapter 6. Metrics

Metrics, it's the one topic you'll see every Developer Relations person talk about. It's often the thing I receive DMs on Twitter about. New departments looking to start and needing help defining their goals and measurements on those goals.

It can be hard to measure what your Developer Relations department does. The core of Developer Relations is building relationship. Having coffee chats with people, speaking to a group of students, or being open to answers questions. These are hard activities to track and often hard to measure.

There are metrics you can track, like video views, or watch time of your videos, how many people attended a talk or how many people clicked on a link.

But are those metrics, showing the success of your department? Are they showing the impact? They are part of the answer, but they aren't the full answer.

Your department, your mission statement, your goals should be about doing the right things. Not just the things that are easy to measure.

Remember though your organisation is paying for the Developer Relations department so they will need to see value out of the department. Don't ignore things that are important to the rest of the business. If your business has a free trial for your product, make sure that is one of your calls to action.

The Sales department take care of the leads and sales pipeline, no one is asking the Developer Relations department to turn into salespeople. But the Developer Relations department should be there to help support the sales team. Help every department within the organisation.

Work towards helping the wider organisational goals, don't ignore them or avoid them.

Chapter 7. So, you want to be an Advocate?

If you are reading this book and looking to become an Advocate within the Developer Relations space, there are things you can do to build up your portfolio and experience.

Create content

Start to create content, start sharing your knowledge with your peers, with people starting out. Build up your catalogue or portfolio of content.

This might mean in your spare time writing blog posts or preparing and giving talks at user groups. It could mean starting a YouTube channel.

Share your knowledge and insights around a specific product or technology.

This will do three things for you:

1. It will start to give you experience creating content and build up your skillset in that area.
2. It will get you noticed by the community, your peers. You'll build up your network, build the community around your own content. This will help open new opportunities for you.
3. You'll also start to understand what the role involves and get a feel for whether it's something you'd like to do full time or not.

I would recommend trying all different types of content creation. You may start to find that you prefer or are even better at certain types of content creation than others.

You don't need to be active in all forms of content creation.

WORK WITH THE COMMUNITY

Get involved in the community, become an active part in it. Take a genuine interest in what's happening in the community. Find the sticking points people have, technical or non-technical and see if you can help. Unblocking those sticking points is essentially what Developer Relations is.

Be genuine about why you are interacting with the community, try things such as:

- Respond to forum posts.
- Share content you've read/watched/listened to that's been helpful.
- Thank people for their contributions.
- Offer advice.
- Ask questions.
- Be curious.
- Help organise user groups.
- Volunteer at conferences.
- Get involved with open-source projects.

Social Media

Love or hate social media is now a method of communication with your community. If you don't already have a social media presence, it's time to think about it.

My advice would be to have a consistent username or handle across all the platforms that you want to be active on. This will help people find you and realise that it's you across the different platforms.

As well as having that consistent username, have the same profile picture, have the same colour scheme, same header image, etc. Again, this helps to identify it's you.

You don't have to have a public profile on every platform though, I have some social media accounts that I don't advertise publicly and are only for family and close friends.

Success on social media won't happen overnight and may even take years to build up but it can be useful and helpful.

Be mindful to build good habits and relationships with the social media platforms, you don't have to have the apps installed on your phone or notifications turned on. You are allowed to not always be switched on to it.

It can be quite pleasing to see your follower count go up, and see the interaction from people, but it isn't healthy constantly checking and associating success with what happens on these platforms so please do build good habits.

RESEARCH

There are lots of online material, blogs, conferences, etc these days that focus on Developer Relations. Search around for those and start your learning journey. Learn more about what others are doing, what strategies they are using, the good the bad and the ugly that comes with Developer Relations.

As much as you need to learn about content creating and building communities you also need to understand about the department and the industry.

Look for others within the space and follow them on social media, reach out to them and see if they have time to answer any of your questions.

Where to go next?

Congratulations on finishing the book! We've come a long way. We've covered off what Developer Relations is, what it isn't, metrics and how to get started.

Hopefully you can take what I have shared in this book with you and go deeper into each area, learning more and trying new things.

Good luck on your journey and please do keep me posted. I'd love to hear if this book helped spark your journey into Developer Relations as a career!

Thanks
- Sarah

About The Author

Sarah Lean is a Senior Technical Specialist at Microsoft. She has worked both at Microsoft and Octopus Deploy as an Advocate and helped to build communities internally and externally at both companies. She now works directly with Azure customers to help with the cloud transition.

With a diverse career that spans over eighteen years, Sarah has been a part of every aspect of the IT world. She began at the start of the industry, working hard at the small jobs until she earned her way to her current position. With determination, Sarah accomplished her goals, getting things done in a timely, intelligent way. This led her to see things on a bigger scope as her passion for technology deepened.

Born and raised on a dairy farm in Scotland, Sarah holds true to her heritage by embracing the natural world through her appreciation for technology. For Sarah, technology is a way to see life as it grows and adapts, ever-changing, just like the natural world of farming.

Sarah is proud to give back to her community. As a STEM Ambassador, Sarah helps others learn how IT can impact and change their lives for the better. Most specifically, she enjoys teaching the next generation of young women how they too can rise in a male-oriented field and succeed in their own careers. Sarah also founded the Glasgow Azure User Group, a community collective who meets bimonthly to network and discuss the latest in technology.

Sarah's enthusiasm in the field of technology has given her the opportunity to speak at public events, most notably, Microsoft Ignite.

You can follow Sarah's blog posts at:
https://www.techielass.com

Or connect with her on Twitter
https://www.x.com/techielass

www.ingramcontent.com/pod-product-compliance
Lightning Source LLC
Chambersburg PA
CBHW072006210526
45479CB00003B/1082